To Daniel: A Sacred Drama by Hannah More

Hannah More was born on February 2nd, 1745 at Fishponds in the parish of Stapleton, near Bristol. She was the fourth of five daughters.

The City of Bristol, at that time, was a centre for slave-trading and Hannah would, over time, become one of its staunchest critics.

She was keen to learn, possessed a sharp intellect and was assiduous in studying. Hannah first wrote in 1762 with The Search after Happiness (by the mid-1780s some 10,000 copies had been sold).

In 1767 Hannah became engaged to William Turner. After six years, with no wedding in sight, the engagement was broken off. Turner then bestowed upon her an annual annuity of £200. This was enough to meet her needs and set her free to pursue a literary career.

Her first play, The Inflexible Captive, was staged at Bath in 1775. The famous David Garrick himself produced her next play, Percy, in 1777 as well as writing both the Prologue and Epilogue for it. It was a great success when performed at Covent Garden in December of that year.

Hannah turned to religious writing with Sacred Dramas in 1782; it rapidly ran through nineteen editions. These and the poems Bas-Bleu and Florio (1786) mark her gradual transition to a more serious and considered view of life.

Hannah contributed much to the newly-founded Abolition Society including, in February 1788, her publication of Slavery, a Poem recognised as one of the most important of the abolition period.

Her work now became more evangelical. In the 1790s she wrote several Cheap Repository Tracts which covered moral, religious and political topics and were both for sale or distributed to literate poor people. The most famous is, perhaps, The Shepherd of Salisbury Plain, describing a family of incredible frugality and contentment. Two million copies of these were circulated, in one year.

In 1789, she purchased a small house at Cowslip Green in Somerset. She was instrumental in setting up twelve schools in the area by 1800.

She continued to oppose slavery throughout her life, but at the time of the Abolition Bill of 1807, her health did not permit her to take as active a role in the movement as she had done in the late 1780s, although she maintained a correspondence with Wilberforce and others.

In July 1833, the Bill to abolish slavery throughout the British Empire passed in the House of Commons, followed by the House of Lords on August 1st.

Hannah More died on September 7th, 1833.

Index of Contents
PERSONS OF THE DRAMA

SCENE
THE SUBJECT
PART I
PART II
PART III
PART IV
PART V
PART VI
PART VII
HANNAH MORE – A SHORT BIOGRAPHY

PERSONS OF THE DRAMA
Darius, King of Media and Babylon.
Pharnaces, Courtier, Enemy to Daniel.
Soranus, dido.
Araspes, A Young Median Lord, Friend and Convert to Daniel
Daniel.

SCENE — The City of Babylon.

THE SUBJECT - Taken from the Sixth Chapter of the Prophet Daniel.

PART I

Pharnaces, Soranus.

Pharnaces
Yes! — I have noted, with a jealous eye,
The pow'r of this new fav'rite! Daniel reigns,
And not Darius! Daniel guides the springs
Which move this mighty empire! High he sits,
Supreme in favour both with prince and people,
Where is the spirit of our Median lords,
Tamely to crouch and bend the supple knee
To this new god? By Mithras, 'tis too much!
Shall great Arbaces' race to Daniel bow—
A foreigner, a captive, and a Jew?
Something must be devised, and that right soon,
To shake his credit.

Soranus
Rather hope to shake
The mountain pine, whose twisting fibres clasp

The earth, deep-rooted. Rather hope to shake
The Scythian Taurus from his central base.
No — Daniel sits too absolute in pow'r,
Too firm in favour, for the keenest shaft
Of nicely aiming jealousy to reach him.

Pharnaces
Rather he sits too high to sit securely.
Yes; he has reach'd that pinnacle of pow'r,
Which closely touches on Depression's verge.
Hast thou then liv'd in courts? hast thou grown gray
Beneath the mask a subtle statesman wears
To hide his secret soul, and dost not know,
That of all fickle Fortune's transient gifts,
Favour in most deceitful? 'Tis a beam,
Which darts uncertain brightness for a moment:
The faint, precarious, sickly shine of power
Given without merit, by caprice withdrawn.
No trifle is so mall as what obtains,
Save that which loses favour: 'tis a breath,
Which hangs upon a smile! A look, a word,
A frown, the air-built tower of fortune shakes,
And down the unsubstantial fabric falls!
Darius, just and clement as he is,
If I mistake not, may be wrought upon
By prudent wiles, by Flattery's pleasant cup,
Administer'd with caution.

Soranus
But the means!
For Daniel's life (a foe must grant him that)
Is so replete with goodness, so adorn'd
With every virtue, so exactly squared
By Wisdom's nicest rules, 'twill be most hard
To charge him with the shadow of offence.
Pure is his fame as Scythia's mountain snows,
When not a breath pollutes them. O Pharnaces,
I've scann'd the actions of his daily life
With all the industrious malice of a foe;
And nothing meets mine eye but deeds of honour
In office pure; for equitable acts
Renown'd: in justice and impartial truth,
The Grecian Themis is not more severe.

Pharnaces
By yon bright sun, thou blazon'st forth his praise,
As if with rapture thou didst read the page
Where these fair deeds are written!

Soranus
Thou mistak'st.
I only meant to show what cause we have
To hate and fear him. I but meant to paint
His popular virtues and eclipsing merit.
Then for devotion, and religious zeal,
Who so renown'd as Daniel? Of his law
Observant in the extreme. Thrice every day,
With prostrate reverence, he adores his God
With superstitious awe his face he turns
Towards his beloved Jerusalem, as if
Some local, partial god might there be found
To hear his supplication. No affair
Of state, no business so importunate,
No pleasure so alluring, no employ
Of such high import, to seduce his zeal
From this observance due!

Pharnaces
There, there he falls!
Enough, my friend! his piety destroys him.
There, at the very footstool of his God,
Where he implores protection, there I'll crush him.

Soranus
What means Pharnaces?

Pharnaces
Ask not what I mean.
The new idea floating in my brain
Has yet receiv'd no form. 'Tis yet too soon
To give it body, circumstance, or breath.
The seeds of mighty deeds are labouring here,
And struggling for a birth! 'Tis near the hour
The king is wont to summon us to council:
Ere that, this big conception of my mind
I'll shape to form and being. Thou, meanwhile,
Convene our chosen friends; for I shall need
The aid of all your counsels, and the weight
Of grave authority.

Soranus
Who shall be trusted?

Pharnaces
With our immediate motive — none, except
A chosen band of friends, who most repine

At Daniel's exaltation. But the scheme
I mediate must be disclosed to all
Who bear high office; all our Median rulers,
Princes and captains, presidents and lords;
All must assemble. 'Tis a common cause;
All but the young Araspes; he inclines
To Daniel and his God. He sits attent,
With ravish'd ears, to listen to his lore:
With reverence names Jerusalem, and reads
The volume of the law. No more he bows
To hail the golden ruler of the day,
But looks for some great Prophet, greater far,
So they pretend, than Mithras! — From him, therefore,
Conceal whate'er of injury is devised
'Gainst Daniel. Be it too thy care, to-day,
To keep him from the council.

Soranus
'Tis well thought.
'Tis now about the hour of Daniel's prayer:
Araspes too is with him: and to-day,
They will not sit in council. Haste we then;
Designs of high importance, once conceived,
Should be accomplish'd. Genius which discerns,
And courage which achieves, despise the aid
Of lingering circumspection. The keen spirit
Seizes the prompt occasion, makes the thought
Start into instant action, and at once
Plans and performs, resolves and executes!

PART II

SCENE — Daniel's House.

Daniel, Araspes.

Araspes
Proceed, proceed, thrice venerable sage,
Enlighten my dark mind with this new ray,
This dawning of salvation. Tell me more
Of this expected King; this Comforter;
This Promise of the nations; this great Hope
Of anxious Israel; this unborn Prophet;
This Wonderful, this mighty Counsellor;
This everlasting Lord, this Prince of Peace;
This Balm of Gilead, which shall heal the wounds

Of universal nature; this Messiah;
Redeemer, Saviour, Sufferer, Victim, God!

Daniel
Enough to animate our faith we know,
But not enough to soothe the curious pride
Of vain philosophy. Enough to cheer
Our path we see, the rest is hid in clouds:
And Heaven's own shadows rest upon the view.

Araspes
Go on, blest sage; I could for ever hear,
Untired, thy admonition. Tell me how
I shall obtain the favour of that God
I but begin to know, but fain would serve.

Daniel
By deep humility, by faith unfeign'd,
By holy deeds, best proof of living faith!
O faith, thou wonder-working principle,
Eternal substance of our present hope,
Thou evidence of things invisible!
What cannot man sustain, sustain'd by thee!
The time would fail, and the bright star of day
Would quench his beams in ocean, and resign
His empire to the silver queen of night:
And she again descend the steep of Heaven,
If I should tell what wonders Faith achieved
By Gideon, Barak, and the holy seer,
Elkanah's son; the pious Gileadite,
Ill-fated Jephthah! He of Zorah, too,
In strength unequall'd; and the shepherd king,
Who vanquish'd Gath's fell giant. Need I tell
Of holy prophets, who, by conquering faith,
Wrought deeds incredible to mortal sense;
Vanquish'd contending kingdoms, quell'd the rage
Of furious pestilence, extinguish'd fire.
Victorious Faith! others by thee endured
Exile, disgrace, captivity, and death?
Some, uncomplaining, bore (nor be it deem'd
The meanest exercise of well-tried Faith)
The cruel mocking, and the bitter taunt,
Foul obloquy, and undeserved reproach;
Despising shame, that death to human pride!

Araspes
How shall this faith be sought?

Daniel
By earnest prayer,
Solicit first the wisdom from above:
Wisdom, whose fruits are purity and peace:
Wisdom, that bright intelligence, which sat
Supreme, when his golden compasses
Th' Eternal plann'd the fabric of the world,
Produced his fair idea into light,
And said that all was good; Wisdom, blest beam
The brightness of the everlasting light;
The spotless mirror of the power of God;
The reflex image of the all-perfect mind;
A stream translucent, flowing from the source
Of glory infinite; a cloudless light;
Defilement cannot touch, nor sin pollute
Her unstain'd purity. Not Ophir's gold,
Nor Ethiopia's gems can match her price;
The ruby of the mine is pale before her;
And, like the oil Elisha's bounty bless'd,
She is a treasure which doth grow by use,
And multiply by spending! She contains,
Within herself, the sum of excellence.
If riches are desired, Wisdom is wealth:
If prudence, where shall keen invention find
Artificer more cunning? If renown,
In her right hand it comes! If piety,
Are not her labours virtues? If the lore
Which sage experience teaches, lo! she scans
Antiquity's dark truths; the past she knows,
Anticipates the future; not by arts
Forbidden, of Chaldean sorcerer,
But from the piercing ken of deep foreknowledge,
From her sure science of the human heart
She weighs effects with causes, ends with means;
Resolving all into the sovereign will.
For earthly blessings moderate be thy prayer,
And qualified; for life, for strength, for grace,
Unbounded thy petition.

Araspes
Now, O prophet!
Explain the secret doubts which rack my mind,
And my weak sense confound. Give my some line,
To sound the depths of Providence! Oh say,
Why the ungodly prosper? why their root
Shoots deep, and their thick branches flourish fair,
Like the green bay tree? why the righteous man,
Like tender plants to shivering winds exposed,

Is stripp'd and torn, in naked virtue bare,
And nipp'd by cruel Sorrow's biting blast?
Explain, O Daniel, these mysterious ways
To my faint apprehension! For as yet
I've much to learn. Fair Truth's immortal sun
Is in itself defective; but obscured
By my weak prejudice, imperfect Faith,
And all the thousand causes which obstruct
The growth of goodness.

Daniel
Follow me, Araspes.
Within thou shalt peruse the sacred page,
The book of life eternal: that will show thee
The end of the ungodly! thou wilt own
How short their longest period; will perceive
How black a night succeeds their brightest day!
Thy purged eye will see God is not slack,
As men count slackness, to fulfil his word.
Weigh well this book; and may the Spirit of grace,
Who stamp'd the seal of truth on the bless'd page,
Descend into thy soul, remove thy doubts,
Clear the perplex'd, and solve the intricate,
Till faith be lost in sight, and hope in joy!

PART III

Darius on his Throne — **Pharnaces, Soranus, Princes, Presidents,** and **Courtiers.**

Pharnaces
Hail, king Darius! live for ever!

Darius
Welcome,
Welcome, my princes, presidents, and friends;
Now tell me, has your wisdom aught devised
To aid the commonwealth? In our now empire,
Subdued Chaldea, is there aught remains
Your prudence can suggest to serve the state,
To benefit the subject, to redress
And raise the injured, to assist th' oppress'd,
And humble the oppressor? If you know,
Speak freely, princes. Why am I a king,
Except to poise the awful scale of justice
With even hand; to 'minister to want;
To bless the nations with a liberal rule,

Vicegerent of th' eternal Oromasdes?

Pharnaces
So absolute thy wisdom, mighty king,
All counsel were superfluous.

Darius
Hold Pharnaces;
No adulation; 'tis the death of virtue:
Who flatters is of all mankind the lowest,
Save he who courts the flattery. Kings are men,
As feeble and as frail as those they rule,
And born, like them, to die. The Lydian monarch,
Unhappy Croesus, lately sat aloft,
Almost above mortality; now see him!
Sunk to the vile condition of a slave,
He swells the train of Cyrus! I, like him,
To misery am obnoxious. See this throne;
This royal throne the great Nebassar fill'd;
Yet hence his pride expelled him. Yonder wall,
The dread terrific writing to the eyes
Of proud Belshazzar shew'd; sad monuments
Of Heaven's tremendous vengeance! And shall I,
Unwarn'd by such examples, cherish pride?
Yet to their dire calamities I owe
The brightest gem that glistens in my crown,
Sage Daniel. If my speech have aught of worth,
Or if my life with aught of good be graced,
To him alone I owe it.

Soranus (aside to **Pharnaces**)
Now, Pharnaces,
Will he run o'er, and dwell upon his praise,
As if we ne'er had heard it; nay, will swell
The nauseous catalogue with many a virtue
His own fond fancy coins.

Pharnaces
O great Darius!
Let thine unworthy servants' words find grace
And meet acceptance in his royal ear,
Who subjugates the East. Let not the king
With anger hear my prayer.

Darius
Pharnaces, speak:
I know thou lov'st me; I but meant to chide
Thy flattery, not reprove thee for thy zeal.

Speak boldly, friends, as man should speak to man.
Perish the barbarous maxims of the East,
Which basely would enslave the freeborn mind,
And plunder man of the best gift of Heaven,
His liberty of soul.

Pharnaces
Darius, hear me.
Thy princes, and the captains of thy bands,
Thy presidents, the nobles who bear rule
O'er provinces, and I, thine humble creature,
Less than the least in merit, but in love,
In zeal, and duty, equal with the first,
We have devised a measure to confirm
Thy infant empire, to establish firmly
Thy power and new dominion, and secure
Thy growing greatness past the power of change.

Darius
I am prepared to hear thee. Speak, Pharnaces.

Pharnaces
The wretched Babylonians long have groan'd
Beneath the rule of princes, weak or rash.
The rod of power has swayed alike amiss,
By feeble Merodach and fierce Belshazzar.
One let the slacken'd reins too loosely float
Upon the people's neck, and lost his power
By nerveless relaxation. He who follow'd,
Held with a tyrant's hand the cruel curb,
And check'd the groaning nation till it bled;
On different rocks they met one common ruin.
Their edicts were irresolute, their laws
Were feebly planned, their councils ill advised;
Now so relax'd, and now so overstrain'd,
That the tired people, wearied with the weight
They long have borne, will soon disdain control,
Tread on all rule, and spurn the hand that guides them.

Darius
But say what remedy?

Pharnaces
That too, O king,
Thy servants have provided. Hitherto
They bear the yoke submissive. But to fix
Thy power and their obedience, to reduce
All hearts to thy dominion, yet avoid

Those deeds of cruelty thy nature starts at,
Thou should'st begin by some imperial act
Of absolute dominion, yet unstain'd
By aught of barbarous. For know, O king!
Wholesome severity, if wisely framed
With sober discipline, procures more reverence
Than all the lenient counsels and weak measures
Of frail irresolution.

Darius
Now proceed
To thy request.

Pharnaces
Not I, but all request it.
Be thy imperial edict issued straight,
And let a firm decree this day be pass'd
Irrevocable as our Median laws.
Ordain that for the space of thirty days,
No subject in thy realm shall aught request
Of God or man, except of thee, O king!

Darius
Wherefore this strange decree?

Pharnaces
'Twill fix the crown
With lasting safety on thy royal brow,
And, by a bloodless means, preserve th' obedience
Of this new empire. Think how much 'twill raise
Thy high renown! 'twill make thy name revered,
And popular beyond example. What!
To be as Heaven, dispensing good and ill
For thirty days! With thine own ears to hear
Thy peoples' wants, with thine own liberal hands
To bless thy supliant subjects! O Darius!
Thou'lt seem as bounteous as a giving god,
And reign in every heart in Babylon
As well as Media. What a glorious state
To be the sovereign arbiter of good;
The first efficient cause of happiness;
To scatter mercies with a plenteous hand,
And to be blest thyself in blessing others.

Darius
Is this the general wish?

[**Princes** and **Courtiers** kneel.]

Chief President
Of one, of all.
Behold thy princes, presidents, and lords,
Thy counsellors, and captains! See, O king!

[Presenting the edict.]

Behold the instrument our zeal has drawn:
The edict is prepared. We only wait
The confirmation of thy gracious word,
And thy imperial signet.

Darius
Say, Pharnaces,
What penalty awaits the man who dares
Transgress our mandate?

Pharnaces
Instant death, O king!
This statute says, 'Should any subject dare
Petition, for the space of thirty days,
Of God or man, except of thee, O king!
He shall be thrown into your dreadful den
Of hungry lions!'

Darius
Hold! Methinks a deed
Of such importance should be wisely weigh'd.

Pharnaces
We have resolved it, mighty king! with care,
With closest scrutiny. On us devolve
Whatever blame occurs!

Darius
I'm satisfied.
Then to your wisdom I commit me, princes,
Behold the royal signet: see, 'tis done.

Pharnaces (aside)
There Daniel fell! That signet seal'd his doom.

Darius (after a pause)
Let me reflect. — Sure I have been too rash!
Why such intemperate haste? but you are wise;
And would not counsel this severe decree
But for the wisest purpose. Yet, methinks,

I might have weigh'd, and in my mind revolved—
This statute, ere, the royal signet stamp'd
It had been past repeal. Sage Daniel too!
My counsellor, my guide, my well-tried friend,
He should have been consulted; he whose wisdom
I still have found oracular.

Pharnaces
Mighty king!
'Tis as it should be. The decree is past
Irrevocable, as the stedfast law
Of Mede and Persian, which can never change,
Those who observe it live, as is most meet,
High in thy grace; — who violate it, die.

PART IV

SCENE— Daniel's House.

Daniel, Araspes.

Araspes
Oh, holy Daniel! prophet, father, friend,
I come the wretched messenger of ill!
Thy foes complot thy death. For what can mean
This new-made law, exorted from the king
Almost by force? What can it mean, O Daniel,
But to involve thee in the toils they spread
To snare thy precious life?

Daniel
How! was the king
Consenting to this edict?

Araspes
They surprised
His easy nature; took him when his heart
Was soften'd by their blandishments. They wore
The mask of public virtue to deceive him.
Beneath the specious name of general good,
They wrought him to their purposes: no time
Allow'd him to deliberate. One short hour,
Another moment, and his soul had gain'd
Her natural tone of virtue.

Daniel

That great Power,
Who suffers evil only to produce
Some unseen good, permits that this should be
And, He permitting, I well pleased resign.
Retire, my friend; this is my second hour
Of daily prayer. Anon we'll meet again.
Here, in the open face of that bright sun
Thy fathers worshipp'd, will I offer up,
As is my rule, petition to our God,
For thee, for me, for Solyma, for all!

Araspes
Oh stay! what mean'st thou! sure thou hast not heard
The edict of the king? I thought, but now,
Thou knew'st its purport. It expressly says,
That no petition henceforth shall be made,
For thirty days, save only to the king;
Nor prayer nor intercession shall be heard
Of any god or man, but of Darius.

Daniel
And think'st thou then my reverence for the king,
Good as he is, shall tempt me to renounce
My sworn allegiance to the King of kings?
Hast thou commanded legions? strove in battle,
Defied the face of danger, mock'd at death
In all its frightful forms, and tremblest now?
Come, learn of me; I'll teach thee to be bold,
Though sword I never drew! Fear not, Araspes,
The feeble vengeance of a mortal man,
Whose breath is in his nostrils; for wherein
Is he to be accounted of? but fear
The awaken'd vengeance of the living Lord;
He who can plunge the everlasting soul
In infinite perdition!

Araspes
Then, O Daniel!
If thou persist to disobey the edict,
Retire and hide thee from the prying eyes
Of busy malice!

Daniel
He who is ashamed
To vindicate the honour of his God,
Of him the living Lord shall be ashamed
When He shall judge the tribes.

Araspes

Yet, oh remember,
Oft I have heard thee say, the secret heart
Is fair Devotion's Temple; there the saint,
Even on that living altar, lights the flame
Of purest sacrifice, which burns unseen,
Not unaccepted. — I remember too,
When Syrian Naaman, by Elisha's hand,
Was cleansed from foul pollution, and his mind
Enlighten'd by the miracle, confess'd
The Almighty God of Jacob; that he deem'd it
No flagrant violation of his fath
To bend at Rimmon's shrine; nor did the Seer
Forbid the rite external.

Daniel

Know, Araspes,
Heaven deigns to suit our trials to our strength,
A recent convert, feeble in his faith,
Naaman, perhaps, had sunk beneath the weight
Of so severe a duty. Gracious Heaven
Forbears to bruise the reed, or quench the flax,
When feeble and expiring. But shall I,
Shall Daniel, shall the servant of the Lord,
A veteran in his cause — long train'd to know
And do his will — long exercised in wo,
Bred in captivity, and born to suffer;
Shall I from known, from certain duty shrink,
To shun a threaten'd danger? O Araspes;
Shall I, advanced in age, in zeal decline?
Grow careless as I reach my journey's end;
And slacken in my pace, the goal in view?
Perish discretion when it interferes
With duty! Perish the false policy
Of human wit, which would commute our safety
With God's eternal honour! Shall His law
Be set at nought, that I may live at ease?
How would the heathen triumph, should I fall
Through coward fear! How would God's enemies
Insultingly blaspheme!

Araspes

Yet think a moment.

Daniel

No!—
Where evil may be done, 'tis right to ponder;
Where only suffer'd, know, the shortest pause

Is much too long. Had great Darius paused,
This ill had been prevented. But for me,
Araspes, to deliberate is to sin.

Araspes
Think of thy power, thy favour with Darius:
Think of thy life's importance to the tribes,
Scarce yet return'd in safety. Live! Oh live!
To serve the cause of God!

Daniel
God will himself
Sustain his righteous cause. He knows to raise
Fit instruments to serve Him. Know, Araspes,
He does not need our crimes to help his cause;
Nor does his equitable law permit
A sinful act from the preposterous plea
That good may follow it. For me, my friend,
The spacious earth holds not a bait to tempt me.
What would it profit me, if I should gain
Imperial Ecbatan, th' extended land
Of fruitful Media, nay, the world's wide empire,
If mine eternal soul must be the price?
Farewell, my friend! time presses. I have stolen
Some moments from my duty, to confirm
And strengthen thy young faith! Let us fulfil
What Heaven enjoins — and leave to Heaven the event.

PART V

SCENE — The Palace.

Pharnaces, Soranus.

Pharnaces
'Tis done — success has crown'd our scheme, Soranus,
And Daniel falls into the deep-laid toils
Our prudence spread.

Soranus
That he should fall so soon,
Astonishes even me! What! not a day?
What! not a single moment to defer
His rash devotions? Madly thus to rush
On certain peril, quite transcends belief!
When happen'd it, Pharnaces?

Pharnaces
On the instant:
Scarce is the deed accomplish'd. As he made
His ostentatious prayer, even in the face
Of the bright God of day, all Babylon
Beheld the insult offer'd to Darius.
For, as in bold defiance of the law,
His windows were not closed, our chosen bands,
Whom we had placed to note him, soon rush'd in
And seized him in the warmth of his blind zeal,
Ere half his prayer was finish'd. Young Araspes,
With all the wild extravagance of grief,
Prays, weeps, and threatens. Daniel silent stands,
With patient resignation, and prepares
To follow them. — But see, the king approaches!

Soranus
How's this? deep sorrow sits upon his brow!
And stern resentment fires his angry eye.

[Enter **Darius**

Darius
O deep-laid stratagem! O artful wile!
To take me unprepared, to wound my heart,
Even where it feels most tenderly, in friendship!
To stab my fame! to hold me up a mark
To future ages, for the perjured prince
Who slew the friend he loved! O Daniel, Daniel,
Who now shall trust Darius? not a slave
In my wide empire, from the Indian main
To the cold Caspian, but is more at ease
Than I, his monarch! Yes! I've done a deed
Will blot my honour with eternal stain!
Pharnaces! O thou hoary sycophant!
Thou wily politician! thou hast snared
Thy unsuspecting master!

Pharnaces
Great Darius,
Let not resentment blind thy royal eyes.
In what am I to blame? Who would suspect
This obstinate resistance to the law?
Who could foresee that Daniel would perforce
Oppose the king's decree?

Darius

Thou, thou foresaw'st it!
Thou knew'st his righteous soul would ne'er endure
So long an interval of prayer. But I,
Deluded king! 'twas I should have foreseen
His stedfast piety. I should have thought
Your earnest warmth had some more secret source,
Something that touch'd you nearer than your love,
Your well feign'd zeal, for me. — I should have known,
When selfish politicians, hackney'd long
In fraud and artifice, affect a glow
Of patriot fervour, or fond loyalty,
Which scorns all show of interest, that's the moment
To watch their crooked projects.— Well thou know'st
How dear I held him! how I prized his truth!
Did I not choose him from a subject world,
Unbless'd by fortune, and by birth ungraced,
A captive, and a Jew? Did I not love him?
Was he not rich in independent worth,
And great in native goodness? That undid him!
There, there he fell! If he had been less great,
He had been safe. Thou could'st not bear his brightness;
The lustre of his virtues quite obscured,
And dimm'd thy fainter merit. Rash old man!
Go, and devise some means to set me free
From this dread load of guilt! Go, set at work
Thy plotting genius to redeem the life
Of venerable Daniel!

Pharnaces
'Tis too late.
He has offended 'gainst the new decree;
Has dared to make petition to his God,
Although the dreadful sentence of the act
Full well he knew. And by the establish'd law
Of Media, by that law irrevocable,
Which he has dared to violate, he dies!

Darius
Impiety! presumption! monstrous law
Irrevocable! Is there aught on earth
Deserves that name? The eternal laws alone
Of Oromasdes are unchangeable!
All human projects are so faintly framed,
So feebly plann'd, so liable to change,
So mix'd with error in their very form,
That mutable and mortal are the same.
But where is Daniel? Wherefore comes he not
To load me with reproaches? to upbraid me

With all the wrongs my barbarous haste has done him?
Where is he?

Pharnaces
He prepares to meet his fate.
This hour he dies, for so the act decrees.

Darius
Suspend the bloody sentence. Bring him hither.
Or rather let me seek him, and implore
His dying pardon and his parting prayer.

PART VI

SCENE — Daniel's House.

Daniel, Araspes.

Araspes
Still let me follow thee; still let me hear
The voice of Wisdom, ere the silver chord
By Death's cold hand be loosen'd.

Daniel
Now I'm ready.
No grief, no woman's weakness, good Araspes!
Thou should'st rejoice my pilgrimage is o'er,
And the blest haven of repose in view.

Araspes
And must I lose thee, Daniel? Must thou die?

Daniel
And what is death, my friend, that I should fear it?
To die! why 'tis to triumph: 'tis to join
The great assembly of the good and just;
Immortal worthies, heroes, prophets, saints!
Oh! 'tis to join the band of holy men,
Made perfect by their sufferings! 'Tis to meet
My great progenitors! 'Tis to behold
Th' illustrious patriarchs; they with whom the Lord
Deign'd hold familiar converse! 'Tis to see
Bless'd Noah, and his children, once a world!
'Tis to behold, oh! rapture to conceive!
Those we have known, and loved, and lost below!
Bold Azariah, and the band of brothers,

Who sought in bloom of youth, the scorching flames!
Nor shall we see heroic men alone,
Champions who fought the fight of faith on earth:
But heavenly conquerors, angelic hosts,
Michael and his bright legions, who subdued
The foes of Truth to join their blest employ
Of love and praise! to the high melodies
Of choirs celestial to attune my voice,
Accordant to the golden harps of saints!
To join in blest hosannahs to their King!
Whose face to see, whose glory to behold,
Alone were Heaven, though saint or seraph none
Should meet our sight, and only God were there!
This is to die! Whou would not die for this?
Who would not die, that he might live for ever?

[**Darius, Daniel, Araspes.**

Darius
Where is he? Where is Daniel? Let me see him!
Let me embrace that venerable form,
Which I have doom'd to glut the greedy maw
Of furious lions!

Daniel
King Darius, hail!

Darius
Oh, injured Daniel! can I see thee thus,
Thus uncomplaining? can I bear to hear,
That when the ruffian ministers of death
Stopp'd thy unfinish'd prayer, thy pious lips
Had just invoked a blessing on Darius,
On him who sought thy life? Thy murderers dropt
Tears of strange pity. Look not on me thus
With mild benignity! Oh! I could bear
The voice of keen reproach, or the strong flash
Of fierce resentment; but I cannot stand
That touching silence, nor that patient eye
Of meek respect.

Daniel
Thou art my master still.

Darius
I am thy murderer! I have sign'd thy death!

Daniel

I know thy bent of soul is honourable:
Thou hast been gracious still! Were it not so,
I would have met the appointment of high Heaven
With humble acquiescence: but to know
Thy will concurr'd not with thy servant's fate,
Adds joy to resignation.

Darius
Here I swear,
By him who sits enthroned in yon bright sun,
Thy blood shall be atoned! One these thy foes
Thou shalt have ample vengeance.

Daniel
Hold, O king!
Vengeance is mine, th' eternal Lord has said:
Myself will recompense, with even hand,
The sinner for the sin. The wrath of man
Works not the righteousness of God.

Darius
I had hoped
We should have trod this busy stage together
A little longer, then have sunk to rest
In honourable age! Who now shall guide
My shatter'd bark in safety? Who shall now
Direct me? Oh, unhappy state of kings!
'Tis well the robe of majesty is gay,
Or who would put it on? A crown! What is it?
It is to bear the miseries of a people;
To bear their murmurs, feel their discontents,
And sink beneath a load of splendid care!
To have your best success ascribed to Fortune,
And Fortune's failures all ascribed to you:
It is to sit upon a joyless height,
To every blast of changing Fate exposed!
Too high for hope! too great for happiness;
For friendship too much fear'd! to all the joys
Of social freedom, and th' endearing charm
Of liberal interchange of soul, unknown!
Fate meant me an exception to the rest,
And, though a monarch, bless'd me with a friend;
And I — have murder'd him!

Daniel
My hour approaches.
Hate not my memory, king: protect Araspes:
Encourage Cyrus in the holy work

Of building ruin'd Solyma. Farewell!

Darius
With most religious strictness I'll fulfil
Thy last request. Araspes shall be next
My throne and heart. Farewell!

[They embrace.

Hear, future kings,
Ye unborn rulers of the nations hear!
Learn from my crime, from my misfortunes learn,
That delegated power which Oromasdes
Invests in monarchs for the public good.

PART VII

SCENE— The Court of the Palace, — The Sun rising.

Darius, Araspes.

Darius
Oh, good Araspes! what a night of horror!
To me the dawning day brings no return
Of cheerfulness or peace! No balmy sleep
Has seal'd these eyes, no nourishment has past
These loathing lips, since Daniel's fate was sign'd!
Hear what my fruitless penitence resolves—
The thirty days my rashness had decreed
The edict's force should last, I will devote
To mourning and repentance, fasting, prayer,
Ad all due rites of grief. For thirty days
No pleasant sound of dulcimer or harp,
Sackbut, or flute, or psaltery, shall charm
My ear, now dead to every note of joy!

Araspes
My grief can know no period!

Darius
See that den!
There Daniel met the furious lions' rage!
There were the patient martyr's mangled limbs,
Torn piecemeal! Never hide thy tears, Araspes!
'Tis virtuous sorrow, unallay'd, like mine,
By guilt and fell remorse! Let us approach;

Who knows but that dread Power to whom he pray'd
So often and so fervently, has heard him!

[He goes to the mouth of the den.

O Daniel! servant of the living God!
He whom thou hast served so long, and loved so well,
From the devouring lion's famish'd jaw
Can he deliver thee?

Daniel (from the bottom of the den)
He can, he has.

Darius
Methought I heard him speak!

Araspes
Oh! wondrous force
Of strong imagination! were thy voice
Loud as the trumpet's blast, it could not wake him
From that eternal sleep!

Daniel (in the den)
Hail! King Darius!
The God I serve has shut the lions' mouths,
To vindicate my innocence.

Darius
He speaks!
He lives!

Araspes
'Tis no illusion; 'tis the sound
Of his known voice.

Darius
Where are my servants! Haste,
Fly, swift as lightning, free him from the den!
Release him, bring him hither! Break the seal
Which keeps him from me! See, Araspes, look!
See the charm'd lions! — mark their mild demeanour!
Araspes, mark! — they have no power to hurt him!
See how they hang their heads, and smooth their fierceness,
At his mild aspect.

Araspes
Who that sees this sight,
Who that in after-times shall hear this told,

Can doubt if Daniel's God be God indeed?

Darius
None, none, Araspes!

Araspes
Ah! he comes, he comes!

[Enter **Daniel,** followed by **Multitudes**

Daniel
Hail, great Darius!

Darius
Dost thou live indeed?
And live unhurt?

Araspes
Oh, miracle of joy!

Darius
I scarce can trust my eyes! how didst thou 'scape?

Daniel
That bright and glorious Being, who vouchsafed
Presence divine when the three martyr'd brothers
Essay'd the cauldron's flame, supported me!
E'en in the furious lions' dreadful den,
The prisoner of hope, even there I turn'd
To the strong hold, the bulwark of my strength,
Ready to hear, and mighty to redeem!

Darius (to **Araspes**)
Where is Pharnaces? take the hoary traitor!
Take too Soranus, and the chief abettors
Of this dire edict! let no one escape
The punishment their deep-laid hate devised
For holy Daniel, on their heads shall fall
With tenfold vengeance. To the lions' den
I doom his vile accusers! All their wives,
Their children too, shall share one common fate;
Take care that none escape. — Go, good Araspes.

[**Araspes** goes out.]

Daniel
Not so, Darius!
Oh spare the guiltless! Spare the guilty too!

Where sin is not, to punish were unjust;
And where sin is, O king, there fell remorse
Supplies the place of punishment!

Darius
No more!
My word is past! Not one request, save this,
Shalt thou e'er make in vain. Approach, my friends;
Araspes has already spread the tale,
And see what crowds advance!

People
Long live Darius!
Long live great Daniel too, the people's friend!

Darius
Draw near my subjects. See this holy man!
Death had no pow'r to harm him.
Of famish'd lions, soften'd at his sight,
Forgot their nature, and grew tame before him.
The mighty God protects his servants thus?
The righteous thus he rescues from the snare!
While fraud's artificer himself shall fall
In the deep gulph hils wily arts devise
To snare the innocent!

A Courtier
To the same den
Araspes bears Pharnaces and his friends.
Fall'n is their insolence! With prayers and tears,
And all the meanness of high-crested pride,
When adverse fortune frowns, they beg for life.
Araspes will not hear. 'You heard not me,'
He cries, 'When I for Daniel's life implored;
His God protected him! see now if yours
Will listen to your cries!'

Darius
Now hear,
People and nations, languages and realms
O'er whom I rule! Peace be within your walls
That I may banish from the minds of men
The rash decree gone out; hear me resolve
To counteract its force by one more just;
In every kingdom of my wide-stretch'd realm,
From fair Chaldea to th' extremest bound
Of northern Media, be my edict sent,
And this my statute known. My heralds, haste,

And spread my royal mandate through the land,
That all my subjecst bow the ready knee
To Daniel's God — for HE alone is Lord.
Let all adore and tremble at his name,
Who sits in glory unapproachable
Above the heavens — above the heaven of heavens?
His power is everlasting; and his throne,
Founded in equity and truth shall last
Beyond the bounded reign of time and space,
Through wide eternity? With his right arm
He saves, and who opposes? He defends,
And who shall injure? In the perilous den
He rescued Daniel from the lions' mouths!
His common deeds are wonders; all his works
One ever-during chain of miracles!

[Enter **Araspes**.

Araspes
All hail, O king! Darius live for ever!
May all thy foes be as Pharnaces is!

Darius
Araspes, speak.

Araspes
Oh, let me spare the tale?
'Tis full of horror! dreadful was the sight!
The hungry lions, greedy for their prey,
Devour'd the wretched princes ere they reach'd
The bottom of the den.

Darius
Now, now confess
'Twas some superior hand restrain'd their rage
And tamed their furious appetites.

People
'Tis true.
The God of Daniel is a mighty god;
He saves and he destroys.

Araspes
O friend! O Daniel!
No wav'ring doubts can ever more disturb
My settled faith.

Daniel

To God be all the glory!

Hannah More was born on February 2nd, 1745 at Fishponds in the parish of Stapleton, near Bristol. She was the fourth of five daughters of Jacob More, a schoolmaster. He was originally from a family of Presbyterians in Norfolk, but had become a member of the Church of England to pursue a career in the Church. After losing a lawsuit over an estate he had hoped to inherit, he moved to Bristol, becoming an excise officer and later a teacher at the Fishponds free school.

The City of Bristol, at that time, was a centre for slave-trading and Hannah would, over time, become one of its staunchest critics.

The More's were a close family and all the sisters were educated at first by their father who taught them Latin and mathematics. Hannah was also taught French by her elder sisters. Her conversational French was improved by time spent with French prisoners of war from the Seven-Year's-War in Frenchay, then a small village near Bristol.

She was keen to learn, possessed a sharp intellect and was assiduous in studying and, according to family tradition, began writing at an early age.

In 1758 Jacob established his own girls' boarding school at Trinity Street in Bristol for the elder sisters, Mary and Elizabeth, to run. Hannah became a pupil there when she was 12. Jacob and his wife moved to Stony Hill in the city to open a school for boys.

Hannah became a teacher at her sister's school and it was here that she produced her first literary efforts. These were prompted by trying to find material suitable for her young charges to act in. Her first, written in 1762, was The Search after Happiness (by the mid-1780s some 10,000 copies had been sold).

In 1767 Hannah gave up her share in the school to become engaged to William Turner. After six years, with no wedding in sight, and Turner reluctant to move forward, the engagement was broken off. It was now 1773 and by all accounts Hannah suffered a nervous breakdown and spent some time recuperating in nearby Uphill. Turner then bestowed upon her an annual annuity of £200. This was enough to meet her needs and set her free to pursue a literary career. With that ambition London was her next stop. She travelled there in the winter of 1773/74 together with her sisters, Sarah and Martha.

She had previously written some verses on a production of King Lear staged by the famous actor David Garrick and this led to a lasting friendship with him and a pivotal introduction to the London Literary society. Now she met and charmed Samuel Johnson, Joshua Reynolds and Edmund Burke. Johnson is quoted as saying to her "Madam, before you flatter a man so grossly to his face, you should consider whether or not your flattery is worth having." He would later be quoted as calling her "the finest versifatrix in the English language".

Hannah also became a leading member of the Bluestocking group of women who met to further literary and intellectual pursuits. Here she met women who were to become life-long friends; Elizabeth

Montagu, Frances Boscawen, Elizabeth Carter, Elizabeth Vesey and Hester Chapone (Hannah later wrote a celebration of this circle in her 1782 poem The Bas Bleu, or, Conversation, published in 1784).

Her first play, The Inflexible Captive, was staged at Bath in 1775. It was based on the opera, Attilio Regulo, by the Italian Pietro Metastasio (1698-1782) whose works she admired.

Her theatrical career was now in full swing. David Garrick himself produced her next play, Percy, in 1777 as well as writing both the Prologue and Epilogue for it. It was a great success when performed at Covent Garden in December of that year. Her next play, Fatal Falsehood, was staged in 1779, shortly after the death of Garrick. It was less successful but still admired.

With David Garrick now passed (January 20th, 1779) Hannah came to view the theatre as both morally wrong and not where her ambitions now lay. She now began to spend her time advancing her interests in other areas.

In 1781 she first met Horace Walpole, man of letters art historian and Whig politician and now corresponded regularly with him.

A friendship with James Oglethorpe, who had long been concerned with slavery as a moral issue and who was working with Granville Sharp in an early abolitionist capacity, started to awaken Hannah's social conscious.

Hannah turned to religious writing, beginning with her Sacred Dramas in 1782; it rapidly ran through nineteen editions. These and the poems Bas-Bleu and Florio (1786) mark her gradual transition to a more serious and considered view of life and are fully expressed in her Thoughts on the Importance of the Manners of the Great to General Society (1788), and An Estimate of the Religion of the Fashionable World (1790).

In Bristol, in 1784, she discovered the poet Ann Yearsley, the so-called 'poetical milkmaid of Bristol'. With Yearsley destitute, Hannah raised a considerable sum of money for her. Lactilia, as Yearsley was known, published Poems, on Several Occasions in 1785, earning about £600. Hannah and Elizabeth Montagu held the profits in trust to protect them from Yearsley's husband. However Ann wished for the capital to be made over, and made insinuations of stealing against Hannah. The money was released and Hannah felt her reputation had been tarnished.

With the death of Samuel Johnson in December 1784, Hannah moved, with her sister Martha, in 1795, to a cottage at Cowslip Green, near Wrington in rural Somerset, "to escape from the world gradually".

In the summer of 1786, she spent time with Sir Charles and Lady Margaret Middleton at their home in Teston in Kent. Among their guests was the local vicar James Ramsay and a young Thomas Clarkson, both of whom were central to the early abolition campaign against slavery.

In 1787, she met John Newton and the 'Clapham Sect' (a group of wealthy evangelical Christians who lived near Clapham and met at Henry Thornton's house). The group was strongly opposed to the Slave Trade. William Wilberforce was a member of the group and he and Hannah became firm friends.

Hannah contributed much to the running of the newly-founded Abolition Society including, in February 1788, her publication of Slavery, a Poem which has long been recognised as one of the most important poems of the abolition period. The poem dramatically described a mistreated, enslaved female separated from her children and severely questioned Britain's role in the Slave Trade.

Her relationship with members of the society, especially Wilberforce, was close. She spent the summer of 1789 holidaying with Wilberforce in the Peak District, planning for the abolition campaign, which, at the time, was at its height.

Her work now became more evangelical. In the 1790s she wrote several Cheap Repository Tracts which covered moral, religious and political topics and were both for sale or distributed to literate poor people. This coincided with her increasing philanthropic work in the Mendip area.

Beyond any doubt, Hannah was the most influential female member of the Society for Effecting the Abolition of the African Slave Trade.

Hannah wrote many ethical books and tracts: Strictures on the Modern System of Female Education (1799), Hints towards Forming the Character of a Young Princess (1805), Cœlebs in Search of a Wife (only nominally a story, 1809), Practical Piety (1811), Christian Morals (1813), Character of St Paul (1815), Moral Sketches (1819). She was a rapid writer, and her work is consequently discursive, animated and without a rigorous structure.

However the originality and force of Hannah's writings perhaps explains her extraordinary popularity. At the behest of Beilby Porteus, Bishop of London and a leading abolitionist, Hannah wrote many spirited rhymes and prose tales, the earliest of which was Village Politics, by Will Chip (1792), intended to counteract the doctrines of Thomas Paine and the influence of the French Revolution.

The series of Cheap Repository Tracts, eventually led to the formation of the Religious Tracts Society. The Tracts were produced at the rate of three a month between 1795 and 1797.

The most famous is perhaps The Shepherd of Salisbury Plain, describing a family of incredible frugality and contentment. Two million copies of these rapid and telling sketches were circulated, in one year, teaching the poor in rhetoric of the most ingenious homeliness to rely upon the virtues of content, sobriety, humility, industry and reverence for the British Constitution, hatred of the French, trust in God and in the kindness of the gentry.

Several of the Tracts oppose slavery and the slave trade, in particular, the poem The Sorrows of Yamba; or, The Negro Woman's Lamentation, which appeared in November 1795 and which was co-authored with Eaglesfield Smith. However, the tracts have also been noted for their encouragement of social quietism in an age of revolution.

In 1789, she purchased a small house at Cowslip Green in Somerset. Wilberforce encouraged Hannah to set up a Sunday school in Cheddar, where poor children could be taught to read. Soon she and her sisters had set up similar schools throughout the Mendip villages, despite fierce opposition.

She was instrumental in setting up twelve schools by 1800 where reading, the Bible and the catechism were taught to local children. Hannah also donated money to Bishop Philander Chase for the founding of Kenyon College, and a portrait of her hangs there in Peirce Hall.

John Scandrett Harford of Blaise Castle was a prodigious benefactor to More's schools in the 1790s, and Hannah modeled the idealised hero and heroine in Cœlebs in Search of Wife (1809) on Mr and Mrs Harford.

However it cannot be said that Hannah was a staunch supporter of Women's rights. She refused to read Mary Wollstonecraft's Rights of Women, saying "so many women are fond of government... because they are not fit for it. To be unstable and capricious is but too characteristic of our sex". She was also shocked by the movement for female education in France, saying "they run to study philosophy, and neglect their families to be present at lectures in anatomy". She is also said to have turned down an honorary membership of the Royal Society of Literature because she considered her "sex alone a disqualification".

The More sisters also met with a good deal of opposition in their philanthropic works: the farmers thought that education, even to the limited extent of learning to read, would be fatal to agriculture, and the clergy, whose neglect she was making good, accused her of Methodist tendencies.

She continued to oppose slavery throughout her life, but at the time of the Abolition Bill of 1807 (which outlawed the slave trade, but not slavery itself), her health did not permit her to take as active a role in the movement as she had done in the late 1780s, although she maintained a correspondence with Wilberforce and others Abolitionists.

In her later life, she continued to dedicate much of her time to religious writing. Nevertheless, her most popular work was a novel, Cœlebs in Search of a Wife, which appeared in two volumes in 1809 (and which ran to nine editions in 1809 alone).

In 1816, Hannah was still at odds with the French. Following Waterloo she is quoted as saying that 'peace with France is a worse evil than war', and refused to allow a French translation of Cœlebs.

Her last few years were spent at Clifton, people from all parts came to visit her even though her health was fading and she was writing less often.

She lived just long enough to see the act finally abolishing slavery. In July 1833, the Bill to abolish slavery throughout the British Empire passed in the House of Commons, followed by the House of Lords on August 1st.

Hannah More died on September 7th, 1833. She is buried at Church of All Saints, Wrington. In her will she left more than £30,000 to charities and religious societies, the equivalent today of many millions.

www.ingramcontent.com/pod-product-compliance
Lightning Source LLC
Chambersburg PA
CBHW060106050426
42448CB00011B/2639